Introduction

We believe that Waitrose Cirencester must be the flagship of the Waitrose fleet, but to us and others it's much, much more….my children call it their 'mother's church' in which I worship most days of the week. I have to concede that they might be right because on Sundays I meet my best friend for therapy, bacon rolls and gossip in the store's café. We are not the only faithful regulars, and this book - which is not a common-or-garden cookbook - will illustrate that Waitrose is not just a top end supermarket, but a truly community store. It will certainly contain recipes that you will want to cook (often using Waitrose's own products) but it will also tell you a bit about some of the local Waitrose characters.

The two of us, both Waitrose fans, have cooked together for more than a decade. We met whilst cooking for someone else, but soon realised that we were complementary cooks. Sally is as sweet as I am spicy, and we soon set up as "Someone to Cook", catering for all manner of functions from raucous rugger club dinners to cocktail parties for the good and grand of the county. One of us is a granny and the other a young mother, so we come from many angles. This will be our first book (but hopefully not the last) working with a Waitrose store, but our second in print. Previously we wrote about a café we ran, which despite its small village location, became a runaway success. Winning awards galore, we were begged to write a cookery book - which we did reluctantly - that became a sell-out. We still get asked for it.

This book has the same ethos - the recipes work, the pictures are real, no fancy studios or lighting, not airbrushed and they do what it says on the tin - enjoy.

Measurements & Acknowledgements

Measurements are given in Metric as well as Imperial – when following a recipe, stick to one or the other. Unless otherwise stated, all teaspoon/tablespoon measurements are level. Egg sizes are given when it affects the end result; where not stated, use whatever you happen to have.

My first is in wine but never in cheese

My second's in beans and also in peas

My third is in instore but never in out

My fourth is in porter and also in stout

My fifth is in roast, not lamb but in pork

My sixth is in spoon, also in fork

My seventh is in sausage, never ever in ham

My eighth is a vowel, do you know who I am?

Abbreviations

- g - gramme
- kg - kilogramme
- ml - millilitre
- oz - ounce
- lb - pound
- fl oz - fluid ounce
- tsp - teaspoon (5ml)
- dssp - dessertspoon (10ml)
- tbsp - tablespoon (15ml)

Sally and I would never have produced or finished this book without the sometimes sadistic motivation of Tim, Sally's handsome husband, and generous time and co-operation given to us from the Cirencester Waitrose team, especially Steve, Richard, Mel and every partner who agreed to talk to us and have their photograph taken – thank you all.

As I have said in a recipe that I think Sally invented, there really is no recipe that hasn't been written and tweaked by cooks galore, but we apologise if we appear to have stolen someone's original. Where we have referenced Waitrose ingredients, some products may only be available in larger branches and subject to availability.

Text Annie Murchie • Photography Sally David • Print – David, Three Counties Print • Design – Paul, Bluefish Creative

Contents

Waitrose Cirencester

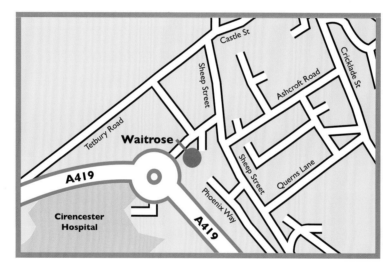

Waitrose Cirencester

Sheep Street • Cirencester • Gloucestershire • GL7 1SZ • Tel. 01285 643733

Standard opening hours
Mon - Thu: 08:30 - 20:00, Fri: 08:30 - 21:00, Sat: 08:30 - 20:00, Sun: 10:00 - 16:00

Company History

Not many people know that the supermarket we all know as Waitrose began life in 1904 on Acton Hill, London, as a small grocery shop. It was started by a Mr Waite, Mr Rose, and for a brief time Mr Taylor. Over 200 stores later, Waitrose still maintains that local ethos. Messrs Waite, Rose and even Taylor would be proud to know that the store they founded is known throughout the UK.

It was 30 odd years later that Waitrose was acquired by John Lewis Partnership, making the supermarket part of its co-owned business. This means that unlike other companies, Waitrose is not governed by Shareholders and the City, but every person or 'Partner', as they are called, who works for the group.

Waitrose assistants are known and talked about for their friendliness and knowledge…maybe it's because of this unique commercial set-up.

Photo courtesy of Waitrose

Leckford Estate

Photo courtesy of Waitrose

I think we all know of Waitrose's commitment to high standards of home grown food - in fact they are one of the few supermarkets that grow some of their own produce. This is done primarily on the Waitrose owned Leckford Estate in Hampshire. The founder of the John Lewis Partnership, John Spedan Lewis bought the farm in 1928 and aimed to use the land to develop new ways of farming that would deliver good quality food, but work in harmony with the environment. The 4,000 acres now includes a farm, plant nursery, water garden, farm shop and Partner residences, but still champions John Spedan Lewis's vision.

The estate has a working farm which grows arable crops, including wheat. Leckford labelled flour is found in most Waitrose branches. Leckford is also one of the farms which supplies Essential Waitrose milk. All the farmers in the dairy scheme share the same values and a commitment to delivering the highest standards, working together to ensure high levels of care for their cattle and the countryside and to promote sustainable farming.

All the pre-packed white mushrooms sold at Waitrose come from Leckford. Available within 24 hours of being picked.

The Leckford fruit farm is fascinating and another testament to John Spedan Lewis. Flying in the face of conventional thinking, he planted the fruit orchard on chalk downland. This proved to be very successful and now produces a number of delicious apple varieties. In addition to the unique flavour that growing on chalk imparts, the apples are crisp and have excellent keeping qualities.

Perhaps the finest accolade of the farm should go to the free-range chickens. There they rear wonderful birds from day-old chicks using traditional husbandry for a minimum of 81 days. Leckford chickens have unlimited daytime access to fields and are fed on a corn-rich diet, free from any added hormones or growth promoters. Their indoor accommodation is a stately home for hens and they reward us by giving us tender, rich and juicy meat.

I could rave at length about this unique farm, but even better, I can send you to see for yourselves. The estate farm shop is open between mid-August and mid-March. Check opening hours by telephoning 01264-810585 - you won't be disappointed!

Light Lunches

This is a selection of starters and
suggestions for light lunches.

Curried Parsnip Soup

Serves 6

75g / 3oz butter

Splash of sunflower oil

1 onion, chopped

1 cooking apple, peeled and chopped

900g / 2lbs parsnips, coarsely grated

1 tbsp plain flour

2 tbsp mild curry paste

1.2 litres / 2 pt hot vegetable stock

1 tbsp mango chutney

1 tbsp apricot jam

To garnish

Cream and coriander leaves

Everyone has their own version of this hearty, warming soup but we honed this recipe until it never fails. Grating the parsnips and adding mango chutney and apple does make a difference.

In a large pan, melt the butter with a little oil (to stop the butter burning). Add the onion, apple and parsnip. Cook slowly for about 10 mins, without colouring, then stir in the flour and curry paste. Gradually incorporate the hot stock, then simmer until the vegetables are cooked.

Stir in the mango chutney and apricot jam. Allow to cool slightly then liquidise until smooth, adding a little water if it's too thick.

Tip
We always use Patak's Mild Curry Paste but never use our best apricot jam.

Jayne's Delicious Mushroom Soup

Serves 6-8

55g / 2oz butter

750g / 1lb 10oz mushrooms (a mixture of chestnut, closed cup and flat)

2 celery stalks

2 leeks

1 large onion

1 20g pack of tarragon

570ml / 1pt. chicken stock (or vegetable stock if catering for vegetarians)

250ml milk

Jayne cooks for the Partners in her immaculate kitchen and is married to Dave, checkout section manager. They've been together for a number of years having first met at a Waitrose fancy dress party.

Roughly chop the onion, celery and leeks and 650g - 1lb 6oz of the mushrooms - then sauté in the butter for 10 minutes. Add stock and milk, then simmer until tender. Cool, then liquidise and add remaining mushrooms with tarragon. Season, reheat and serve.

Pea & Mint Soup

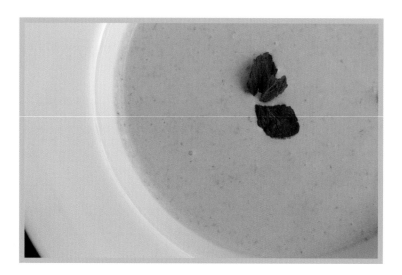

Serves 6-8

55g / 2oz Butter

1 tbsp olive oil

4 spring onions

1 bag 907g / 2 lb frozen essential Waitrose garden peas

1 litre / 1³/₄ pt. vegetable stock

1x 20g pack fresh mint (save a few leaves for garnishing)

1 tsp sugar and a good sprinkling of salt and pepper

150ml / ¹/₄ pt. single cream

This is the lazy last-minute "what can I cook for lunch?" soup.   Most of the ingredients you may have, and you can serve it hot or cold.

Cook off the chopped spring onions in the butter and 1tbsp olive oil until soft.   Add peas (no need to defrost) and mint. Dilute with vegetable stock, bring to simmering point, add salt, pepper and the sugar. Watch carefully as overcooking at this stage will lose the lovely green colour of this soup. Liquidise and add cream (if you aren't a cholesterol worrier) – if you are, OK then, have it as it is or let down with more stock. Garnish with a whole mint leaf.

Cheese Scones

Serves 8

225g / 8oz self-raising flour

3/4 tsp baking powder

1/2 tsp dry mustard

1/2 tsp mixed herbs

50g / 2oz butter, softened

50g / 2oz strong Cheddar, grated

25g / 1oz Parmesan, grated

1 egg, made up to 150ml / 1/2 pt. with milk or buttermilk

We are putting this recipe with the soups because if cut into mini scones they are a delicious accompaniment to any of the soups - do try them....

Preheat oven to 200°C/400°F/Gas Mark 6. Line a baking sheet with baking parchment. Sift the flour, baking powder and mustard into a large bowl. Stir in the mixed herbs and season with salt and pepper. Rub in the butter until the mixture resembles fine breadcrumbs (you can use a freestanding mixer). Add the two grated cheeses, reserving some for sprinkling on the top. Beat together the egg and milk/buttermilk and add most of the liquid to the rubbed-in mixture. Mix to form a soft (but not sticky) dough, adding more liquid as necessary. Turn out onto a floured surface and roll or press out to a thickness of 2cm/3/4 inch. Cut into rounds with a 5cm/2 inch cutter and brush the tops with any liquid left in the jug. Sprinkle with the reserved grated cheese. Bake for 15-20 mins until golden. Transfer to a wire rack to cool.

Black Pudding Delight

Serves 4-6

1 ring of black pudding from the deli counter

3 medium sized leeks, chopped

1 smallish cooking apple, peeled and diced

1 tbsp fresh thyme (dried is ok but use 1tsp.)

3 tbsp olive oil

4 tbsp balsamic vinegar

Black pudding brings only passionate reactions; a bit like Marmite, love it or hate it. If you love it, use this recipe; if not, forget it….

Steam the leeks and set aside. Gently fry the diced apple in the olive oil. When the apple is feeling almost soft, toss in the sliced black pudding and fry for about 10 minutes turning all the time. Add the leeks and balsamic vinegar with the chopped thyme. Move about until the leeks are nice and warm, adding a little more vinegar if the mixture looks dry. Serve with crusty bread and you will love it.

Keith recommends

Beaujolais Villages

Cotswold Rarebit

Serves 6

50g / 2oz strong Cheddar, grated

50g / 2oz Parmesan, grated

50g / 2oz Double Gloucester, grated

50g / 2oz cream cheese

2 tbsp Waitrose Organic Beer

1 large egg yolk

1 tbsp double cream

1 tsp Dijon mustard

2 tsp Worcester sauce

To serve

Toast of your choice

When we discovered the great selection of grated cheese in the Waitrose cheese fixture we jumped for joy. Apart from the convenience of it, the ready grated stuff saves bits of grated finger ending in the mix. In hard times of course you can use the odds and ends of cheese in your fridge.

The rarebit demands a very hot grill, so in the confines of our small café kitchen we only ever had it on the menu after the clocks went back in October for fear of melting the cook. However, a domestic grill is not so fierce and doesn't have to stay on all day, so this can be a delicious lunch or supper dish all year round...and it makes a marvellous canapé on a small croute with a dab of jalapeno chutney on the top.

Preheat the grill to its highest setting.

Make the toast and leave to go cold, preferably in a toast rack or propped up against something so it doesn't go soggy. For the rarebit, combine all the ingredients in a freestanding mixer or food processor. Spread the mixture on the toast. Grill until golden and bubbling.

Tips

We know it sounds a little odd to use cold toast, but it really does seem to work better that way! Our favourites for toast are Ciabatta or Focaccia from the bread counter.

Any leftover rarebit mixture keeps well - allow to cool, then store, covered, for 3 to 4 days in the fridge.

Leftover beer should be swigged back or drunk with the rarebit.

Leek & Prawn Crumble

Serves 6-8

8 leeks, sliced and steamed

*500g / 1 lb prawns
(frozen or fresh)*

*500ml / 1 pt. good cheese
sauce or Waitrose ready
made.*

*150g / 5oz stale
breadcrumbs*

*50g / 2oz grated cheese
(strong Cheddar or
Parmesan)*

2 spring onions, chopped

*Clove of garlic chopped
(optional)*

1 tbsp chopped parsley

50g / 2oz soft butter

This is a most adaptable dish, you can cover almost anything with the crumble mixture. We have done it with roasted vegetables, ratatouille and ham and leeks. It freezes well and a green salad is all you need for an accompaniment.

Mix leeks and prawns together and cover with cheese sauce in a gratin dish.
In a bowl mix the breadcrumbs, cheese, spring onions, garlic and parsley. Rub in the butter. Sprinkle over the leeks and prawns and bake in oven 180°C/350°F/Gas Mark 4 for 40 – 45 minutes.

Keith recommends
Alsace Pinot Gris

Melon, Prawn & Cucumber Salad

Serves 8

1 small melon (cantaloupe, charentais or galia)

1 small cucumber

400g / 14oz cooked large prawns frozen or fresh from the counter

1 x 20g pack fresh mint, finely chopped

4 tbsp vinaigrette dressing See below

Vinaigrette

Makes approx 450ml / 3/4 pt.

75ml / 3fl oz white wine vinegar

1 heaped tsp Dijon mustard

1 heaped tsp caster sugar

Salt and black pepper

275ml / 10fl oz olive oil

1/2 clove garlic, chopped (optional)

Using a melon-baller, scoop the melon into balls and put in a bowl. Peel the cucumber, dice neatly and add to the melon balls. Throw in the prawns (you can use frozen, defrosted ones quite happily) and cover all these ingredients with the minty vinaigrette. If you want to look flash and impress, this can be served in hollowed-out melons. Chill well before serving.

Vinaigrette
Mix the vinegar, mustard, sugar, salt and pepper in a large bowl. Slowly add the olive oil, continually whisking until well blended. It will be quite thick. Add the garlic if using. Pour into a bottle and store in a cool place. Shake well before using.

Moon Blush

Here is her "Moon Blush":

200g / 7oz cherry tomatoes

1 bag rocket leaves

200g / 7oz feta

Olive oil

Fresh thyme

Salt

Zena, of Book Club fame, and a regular customer in Waitrose Cirencester, is not just the cerebral face of the club; she also cooks like a professional – (she sometimes cheats – see "they'll never know" later).

She also has the best quote from the customer questionnaire:

Why do you shop at Waitrose? – "Because it is small enough for me to know exactly where everything is and large enough to have everything I need".

Cover a baking tray with cherry tomatoes, cut in half, drizzle with olive oil and sprinkle with fresh thyme and salt.
Bake in a very low oven 140°C/275°F/Gas Mark 1 for 3 – 4 hrs, or overnight in the bottom of the Aga.

Serve it with a salad of feta and rocket, or on hot pasta.

Trio of Quiches

Makes one 23cm/9 inch quiche

225g / 8oz shortcrust pastry or pack of ready made

3 large eggs

3 large egg yolks

450ml / ³/₄ pt. double cream

A trio of our most popular quiches, but you can invent your own combinations. It is always said that, "real men don't eat quiche"....but we have never seen any evidence of the truth of this saying, especially when we had Stilton and leek on the menu. Try any of these combinations, but don't be mean with the ingredients and see for yourselves.

Preheat oven to 200°C/400°F/Gas Mark 6. Roll out the pastry and line a 23cm/9 inch round quiche tin. Prepare your chosen filling and use to fill the pastry case, as detailed below. Beat together the eggs, egg yolks and cream and pour over the filling. Bake for 40-45 mins until risen, golden and just set in the middle.

French Onion

Slice 4 onions and 1 bunch of spring onions. Warm 2 tbsp oil and 15g/¹/₂ oz butter in a frying pan. Add the two types of onion, 1 tsp chopped fresh thyme and 1 tsp sugar. Fry until golden then allow to cool. Sprinkle 110g/4oz grated Gruyère in the pastry case. Top with the onions and 50g/2oz grated Parmesan. Sprinkle with chopped fresh parsley.

Roasted Vegetables & Goats' Cheese

Chop into bitesized pieces 1 red pepper, 1 yellow pepper, 1 courgette, ¹/₂ aubergine and 2 red onions. Place in a roasting tin and toss with 3 tbsp olive oil. Roast for 30-40 mins until tender. Allow to cool then arrange in the pastry case. Top with 175g/6oz crumbled goats' cheese, some torn basil leaves and a few stoned olives.

Stilton & Leek

Slice 2 leeks and steam until tender. Allow to cool. Sprinkle 25g/1oz grated Cheddar over the pastry base and top with the sliced leeks. Crumble 110g/4oz Stilton over the top.

Salad of Blue Cheese & Pears
with a raspberry vinaigrette

Serves 6 as a starter

*175g / 6oz blue cheese
(Roquefort if you are
feeling flush)*

*3 large ripe pears
thinly sliced*

*1 bag of Waitrose spinach
and watercress salad*

*1 tbsp chopped walnuts
(you can leave these out if
you are worried by allergic
guests)*

*Vinaigrette dressing
(but made with raspberry
vinegar) see page 15*

On individual plates divide the salad and
arrange the pears with the crumbled
cheese on top. Sprinkle with nuts, if using
them, and just before serving, spoon
over the dressing.

Rumour has it that this is the meal that
Blair and Brown had when brokering the
leadership deal. Beware of what you wish
for, Mr Brown…

Smoked Fish Pate

Serves 4-6

225g / 8oz smoked salmon or smoked mackerel fillets

75g / 3oz full-fat cream cheese

1 tbsp lemon juice

1 dssp good mayonnaise

Smoked Salmon Pâté

$1/2$ tsp finely chopped dill

Smoked Mackerel Pâté

1 tbsp creamed horseradish

To serve

Wedge of lemon

Crusty bread or toast

See if you can make a starter quicker than this. Whizz all of the ingredients in a food processor (including the dill for the Smoked Salmon Pâté or creamed horseradish for the Smoked Mackerel Pâté) until smooth but still with some texture. Serve with a wedge of lemon and crusty bread or toast.

Tips
For the Smoked Mackerel Pâté, we always try to include at least one peppered smoked mackerel fillet. For the Smoked Salmon Pâté, it's perfectly OK to use trimmings.

Sweet Potato Galettes with Soft Cheese

1 packet of puff pastry
(ready rolled is fine)

5 cooked and sliced
sweet potatoes

250g / 8oz Taleggio, brie
or goats cheese

6 tbsp green pesto
(fresh is best)

Handful of pumpkin seeds

Olive oil

Roll out the pastry and, depending on your preference, cut into squares or rectangles, size depending on whether it is going to be a starter or light lunch.

Lightly score a 2cm/³/₄ inch border round the edge of the pastry and prick the middle with a fork.

Bake in oven at 200°C/400°F/Gas Mark 6 until lightly browned. When cool scoop out any bits of soggy pastry in the middle, but leave a good base. Lightly spread with pesto, layer the potatoes neatly on the top and cover with your choice of cheese (Taleggio is our favourite): Drizzle with a little olive oil and sprinkle with pumpkin seeds – at this stage you can leave the little darlings. When ready to serve, put on a baking sheet and cook at 180°C/350°F/Gas Mark 4 for 15 - 20 minutes or until the cheese is hot and melting.

Serve with salad leaves and vinaigrette.

Coarse Country Terrine

Serves a good 10

2 pork fillets
(approx 280g / 10oz each)

225g / 8oz pig's liver

225g / 8oz streaky bacon

1 medium onion, chopped finely

1 clove garlic, chopped

3 tbsp olive oil

Splash of brandy (to deglaze pan)

55g / 2oz chopped pitted prunes

55g / 2oz pistachios

1 tsp dried mixed herbs

8-10 more rashers of streaky bacon to line tin

We have been making this recipe for years and we are reliably told it is a mainstay dish for some foodies in France.

Preheat oven to 180°C/350°F/Gas Mark 4. In a food processor chop the pork, liver and bacon (but not too finely) then place in a large bowl. Gently cook the onion and garlic in the olive oil without colouring, until soft – add to the minced meat. Place the frying pan back on to the heat and deglaze it with the brandy. Put in the meat mixture along with the prunes, nuts and mixed herbs – mix well, seasoning as you go.

Line a 2lb/900g loaf tin with the extra rashers of bacon and pack in the pâté. Cover with foil and bake in a bain-marie for 1¹/₂ hours. Cool with a heavy weight and serve in slices with a good chutney and some crusty bread.

Toasted Goats Cheese
with sesame seeds

Serves 6

6 small goats cheeses (or cut big ones)

6 slices of toast – cut in a round, a bit bigger than the cheese

Salad leaves – dressed

50g / 2oz sesame seeds

6 dssp of redcurrant jelly or mango chutney

Heat oven to 200°C/400°F/Gas Mark 6.
Roll the cheese in the seeds – try and
cover the sides completely. Place the circles
of toast on a baking tray, spread with jelly or
chutney and top with goats cheese. Bake
for about 10 minutes or until the cheese
looks as if it is about to melt.
Place on top of the salad leaves which you
have tossed in vinaigrette dressing (see
page 15). Radicchio leaves look good, as
you can nestle the toast in them if they are
the right size.

Mains

Just some of our most tried-and-tested favourites that we
have been asked for, and some that we haven't because
they were contributed by customers and partners.
We have cooked, tasted and photographed them all and
none are airbrushed or painted with castor oil to make
them more photogenic.

Coq Au Vin

Serves 6

12 chicken thighs (not filleted) coated in flour

Lardons – 1pkt.

3 tbsp olive oil

75ml / 3fl oz cognac

425ml / 3/4 pt. chicken stock

570ml / 1pt. full-bodied red wine

1 tbsp tomato puree

2 cloves mashed garlic

1 tbsp fresh thyme or 1 tsp of dried

12 shallots, braised in a little wine and some stock

225g / 8oz button mushrooms

Parsley to garnish

Very Sixties we know, but it never fails to impress. We've served it at a wedding for 200 on a boiling hot August and they still loved it.

In a casserole sauté the lardons in a little oil until lightly browned - set aside. Brown the floured chicken pieces in hot oil, add the lardons and cook slowly for about 10 minutes. Now for the exciting bit - fire extinguishers at the ready - pour in the cognac, turn your face away and light the cognac (with a taper is best). Shake back and forth until the flames die down. Pour the wine into the casserole and add just enough stock to cover the chicken.
Stir in the tomato puree, garlic and herbs. Bring to simmering point, cover and simmer slowly for about 1 hour or until the chicken is cooked. While the chicken is cooking, sauté the mushrooms in a little butter and set aside. In another pan braise the shallots in a little wine and some stock (it is easier to peel the onions if you have soaked them in boiling water).

If you feel that the chicken cooking liquid is not thick enough, now is the time to make a paste with 25g/1oz flour and 25g/1oz butter and whisk into the liquid.

Assemble together the chicken, mushrooms and shallots in your casserole, decorate with parsley and serve. We do it straight from the casserole with a green salad and Dauphinoise potatoes.

Navarin of Lamb

Serves 6

1.35kg / 3lbs lamb, diced
(shoulder is sweetest)

1 tbsp olive oil

1 tbsp granulated sugar

25g / 1oz flour

Salt and pepper

18 new potatoes

6 peeled carrots – little ones
are easy

6 peeled turnips, again those
mini ones are great

12 peeled shallots

570ml / 1 pt. beef stock – a
tin of consommé is perfect
made up with water to 1pt.

3 tbsp tomato puree

2 cloves garlic, mashed

1 tsp thyme or rosemary

225g / 8oz frozen peas

This is a lamb stew with a posh name, but once you have made it you will use it again and again because it is so cook friendly and it leaves you free to enjoy your guests.

Place shallots in a small pan with a little of the beef stock and gently simmer for 10 minutes - then keep to one side. In a frying pan brown the lamb in a very little oil and then place in a biggish casserole. Sprinkle the lamb with sugar (this is the secret of the recipe so do not be tempted to skip it) and stir on the heat until the sugar has caramelized (about 4 minutes). Now add the flour to the pan and toss the meat with the salt and pepper. Place casserole uncovered in the preheated oven (220°C /425°F/Gas Mark 7) for about 5 minutes to brown the flour and coat the lamb with a light crust. Remove casserole and turn oven down to 180°C/350°F/Gas Mark 4. Add consommé and tomato puree to the casserole along with thyme, rosemary and squashed garlic. If the liquid does not cover the meat, add hot water to make it do so. Add peeled and cooked shallots. Return casserole to oven with lid on and leave to cook for 1^{1}/2 - 2 hrs. or longer.   While the lamb is cooking, lightly steam the new potatoes, peas, carrots and turnips - strain. Add to the casserole for at least 5 minutes - relax and wait for the inevitable praise.

Nikki's Pork Fillet with Bacon & Apples

Serves 4

2 pork fillets, trimmed

8 rashers of streaky bacon

4 cooking apples

A few sage leaves

Salt and pepper

275ml / ¹/₂ pt. dry cider

2 tbsp of single cream

My best friend Nikki is an oxymoron; she is a posh Essex girl who caters for the grand of East Anglia. She was always envious of my local Waitrose when she had to travel miles to indulge herself, but last week her dreams came true and they opened one in Colchester. I cannot name the supermarket that has lost her forever.

Preheat oven to 170°C/325°F/Gas Mark 3. Peel, core and slice the apples and put in an ovenproof casserole dish.   Mix in some sage leaves and salt and pepper. Cut the pork fillets into two and wrap each piece in two rashers of bacon.   Place these on top of the apples, pour the cider around. Cook in the oven for about 35 - 40 minutes basting several times. Remove fillets and stir in the cream.

When serving, slice the pork fillets 1cm thick and arrange on the plate with the sauce and fresh sage. Good on mustard mash with a green vegetable.

Posh Fish Pie

Serves 8

750g / 1lb 10oz Fish – cod, haddock, monkfish, salmon

570ml / 1 pt. milk, or combination of milk and single cream

1 glass white wine

75g / 3oz butter

75g / 3oz plain flour

350g / 12oz tiger prawns, cooked

200g / 7oz smoked salmon (use trimmings)

2 tbsp chopped fresh dill

Salt and pepper

8 cooked quails eggs (optional)

Topping

900g / 2lbs potatoes, peeled

60g / 2¹/₂ oz butter

Slurp of cream

Breadcrumbs

Grated cheddar

Preheat oven to 180°C/350°F/Gas Mark 4. Cook the 750g of cod, etc., in the milk and wine for approximately 15 minutes. When the fish is cooked take it out of the baking dish - you are going to use the liquid for the sauce. Melt the butter and add the plain flour, cooking for about 1 minute before adding the liquid from the cooked fish. Simmer until you have a smooth sauce then add the fish, prawns, smoked salmon, dill, salt, pepper and halved quails eggs. Spoon all this mixture into a large gratin dish or individual dishes and leave to cool while you make the topping.

Boil the potatoes and then mash with butter and cream. Cover the fish with the mashed potato and leave it rough if you are like Annie - pipe it prettily if you are like Sally.

Optional: Scatter breadcrumbs and grated cheese on top.

Sit on a baking tray, bake for about 30 minutes 180°C/350°F/Gas Mark 4 until the top is brown and the bottom bubbling - serve with a salad or some mange tout.

Keith recommends
Australian Riesling

Karen & Richard's Chicken Curry

Serves 2-3

1 dssp vegetable oil

1 large onion diced

6 garlic gloves (4 crushed, 2 finely sliced)

2 red chillies chopped seeds optional

1 tsp each of garam masala and ground cumin

1/2 tsp each of ground coriander and ground turmeric

1 1/2 dssp Tandoori curry paste

5cm fresh ginger grated

1 tin chopped tomatoes (400g)

1 dssp tomato purée

2 dssp mango chutney

1 vegetable stock cube

2 boneless and skinless chicken breasts cut into 2cm cubes

Fresh coriander to garnish

I am not prepared to divulge the name of my friend who always refers to Richard Moverley as sex on legs and she hasn't seen him in his leathers! Who would guess that the suave man in a suit has this other side to his company persona. He and his other half, Karen, also a Waitrose Newbury girl are mad about music festivals and food - the spicier the better. We persuaded them to yield their favourite curry recipe - it's good, very good, but beware of the heat.

Preheat oven to 180°C/350°F/Gas Mark 4. Heat oil in a pan or wok, add all the spices and fry for 1 minute. Add onion, crushed garlic, chilli and ginger. Cook until the onions are soft. Add the mango chutney, tomato purée, vegetable stock cube, curry paste and tinned tomatoes. Cook for a further 2 minutes. Pour mixture into a blender or food processor and blitz for 1 minute or until smooth. Taste, add more spices and salt and pepper, if required. Pour mixture into an ovenproof dish, stir in chicken and sliced garlic. Cover and cook for 25 minutes. Add freshly chopped coriander and cook for a few more minutes.

Serve with rice, naan bread and a good Shiraz.

Risotto *of Butternut Squash, Spinach & Goats Cheese*

Serves 8

1 butternut squash, cubed and roasted

1 bag of (salad) spinach

Goats cheese, either a pyramid or 175g / 6oz from the cheese counter

2 pts. stock (vegetable or chicken), hot if possible

2 tbsp olive oil

50g / 2oz butter

4 spring onions, chopped finely

400g / 14oz risotto rice

About 2 wineglasses white wine

(optional, 3 tbsp single cream – see Tip)

For colour and impact you won't beat this combination but you can use the basic risotto recipe and add your own choice of ingredients.

In a large frying pan or wok, gently sauté the spring onions in the olive oil. Cook slowly until soft then add the rice. Turn up the heat. Now begins the serious bit - when the rice looks translucent (about 5 minutes) add the wine and keep stirring. Keep adding spoonfuls of stock until the rice is cooked (this will probably be about 20 minutes - you mustn't answer the telephone or do anything that takes you away from your stirring). Now is the time to add your other ingredients. Stir in the butter and then add the butternut squash and

spinach - the spinach will cook quickly in the heat of the risotto. Before serving, crumble the goat's cheese over the rest - serve immediately, but….

Tip

If there was a crisis at this point you could set the risotto aside and even leave it in the fridge until next day.   Then in a deepish frying pan heat up the 3tbsp cream with a little wine and stir in the risotto - good as fresh.

Steve Gardiner
Branch Manager

I have loved Steve Gardiner, the Cirencester branch manager, ever since he stood up to me on one of my bad reactionary days. He said that if Waitrose listened to the likes of me they would still be selling sugar in blue bags and butter would be patted with wooden pats – touché!   Since then I have been his biggest (sometimes literally!) fan. His heart is as big as his chest measurement and I have witnessed this gentle giant being lovely to little old ladies. I often wondered where this cracker of a manager got that gift from. Writing this book gave me the opportunity to ask him.

It seems that after some years in the hotel industry there came a moment when he had to evaluate his career and decide which bits of the hospitality business he liked most. Luckily for Waitrose that decision led him into retail. Having been at the company for 13 years, the last 7 have been at Waitrose Cirencester. With all his expertise it is not surprising that as well as managing the Cirencester store he also helps the company in assessing future management trainees and is coach and mentor to aspiring new Branch Managers. His recipe for Wellington roulade is well worth trying – the "wiggly beans" are ordinary French beans but described as wiggly worms to persuade one of his daughters to eat her greens.

Big Steve's Wellington Roulade

Serves 4

4 sirloin steaks (Aberdeen Angus or Hereford), flattened and tenderized

2 onions finely chopped

2 cloves of garlic, finely chopped

250g / 8oz Portabella mushrooms finely chopped

125g / 4oz Paté (I like Belgium farm assured coarse paté with peppercorns)

1 litre / 1³/₄ pts whipping cream

110g / 4oz Roquefort

Gently cook the onion and garlic and set aside. Fry the mushrooms until the juices have disappeared, then add half of the onion mixture. Spread the paté onto the steak, followed by the duxelle of mushrooms. Roll each steak into a roulade and secure with string. Fry the roulades in a pan to seal and then bake for 10 minutes at 190°C/375°F/Gas Mark 5, or longer if you prefer it more well done.

To Serve
Heat the remaining onions and garlic with the brandy. Add cream and simmer until reduced by half. Season, then melt the Roquefort into the sauce.

Spoon the sauce on each plate, top with sliced roulade and serve with crunchy roast potatoes (see tip), chantenay carrots, wiggly beans and a good Shiraz.

Tip
To make the roast potatoes really crunchy, parboil for 5 minutes, drain, return to saucepan and lightly cover with semolina. Half way through roasting, add whole sage leaves, sprigs of rosemary and sliced garlic.

Tarragon Chicken

Serves 6

6 chicken breasts, skin off

300ml / 10 fl oz double cream

150ml / 5 fl oz white wine

1 pkt fresh tarragon

2 spring onions, chopped very small

50g / 2oz butter

We got great publicity for this dish at the café. It was raved about in the press when the circus came to town.
It is very easy - here it is.

Poach chicken breasts in a little water with a few sprigs of tarragon and seasoning, simmer for 25 minutes - set aside.
Sauté the spring onions in the butter.
Add the wine and simmer for a few minutes.
Pour in the cream with half of the poaching liquid, let simmer until it has thickened and coats the back of a spoon. Add chopped tarragon. That is it - easy sauce. Slice and add the chicken and warm through.
New potatoes are good with this.

Keith recommends
French Viognier

Puddings

Not for the dieters, mostly quite
calorific – ignore them if you
can, but if you can't, enjoy
without guilt.

Barbados Cream

This recipe pops up in various guises but we think it is worth including as it is so easy and no one can really identify it.

Equal amounts of Waitrose double cream and thick Total Greek yoghurt

Dark muscavado sugar

Soft fruit (optional)

Whisk double cream until thick. Fold in the yoghurt then pour into ramekin dishes - cover top with a thickish layer of dark sugar and put in fridge (best overnight but not vital).

We often use a glass bowl and layer the creamy mixture with the sugar and fruit. As you can see, it looks impressive.

Bread & Butter Pudding with Whisky sauce

Serves 8 All men love this pudding

Pkt. of individual brioche or 1 loaf-shaped brioche

570ml / 1 pt. of double cream plus 300ml / ¹/₂ pt. of milk

3 beaten eggs plus 2 yolks

110g / 4oz caster sugar

110g / 4oz sultanas

200g / 7oz pecan nuts

1 tsp of vanilla essence

Butter for spreading

Whisky sauce:

300ml / 10fl oz single cream

3 egg yolks

1 tbsp caster sugar

1 tsp cornflour

3 tbsp whisky

Preheat the oven to 170°C/325°F/Gas Mark 3. Rub the butter around large ovenproof baking dish. Layer the sliced brioche (which you have buttered) in the dish, with nuts and sultanas between each layer.

Mix cream, milk, eggs, sugar and vanilla essence and pour over the brioche. Push it down if you have to - you need it all to be submerged. Let it stand for 30 minutes in an ideal world, but this is not vital.

Cover with foil (loosely as it will rise).

Place in the oven and bake for 30 minutes. Take off the foil and then cook for another 20 - 30 minutes until golden on top.

Serve with whisky sauce.

Whisky Sauce
Heat the cream very gently over a low heat. Whilst this is happening, whisk the egg yolks, sugar and cornflour together in a basin.

When the cream has reached boiling point pour it onto the egg mixture, whisking as you pour. Return the mixture to the saucepan and put back on the gentle heat and whisk until thick. Stir in whisky and serve.

Chocolate Cheesecake

Base

225g / 8oz chocolate digestives

65g / 2.5oz butter

Topping

450g / 1lb curd cheese

75g / 3oz cater sugar

3 medium eggs

175g / 6oz plain chocolate 70%

1 tbs warm water

2 tbs cornflour

150ml / 1/4 pt. sour cream

Sandra used to run the twilight shift on the cheese counter most nights of the week and, apart from her wide dairy knowledge, is famous for her cheesecake. We have persuaded her to give us the recipe. It is called for whenever there's a Waitrose celebration and we guarantee it will be a winner in everyone's repertoire. Here it is:

Heat oven to 170°C/375°F/Gas Mark 3. Grease and line base of 20cm/8in spring clip tin, place biscuits in a plastic bag and crush until crumbled. Melt the butter and add to the crumbs. Spoon them into the tin and press down with a potato masher.
Chill the base in the fridge while you make the topping. Melt the chocolate and add the water. Place the curd cheese and sugar in a bowl and beat well until smooth. Add the eggs, one at a time, beating well after each addition, then beat in the chocolate. Beat in the sour cream and then the cornflour. Remove the chilled biscuit base from the fridge, pour over the topping mixture. Place on a baking sheet in the centre of the oven for about 35 - 40 mins, until the mixture has just set. Turn off the oven and leave inside with the door slightly open for 30 - 40 mins.

To remove from the tin, run a knife dipped in hot water round the edge, then unclip the side. Leave in the fridge to go cold, then slide a long knife between the base and the lining. To cut up, dip a knife into hot water and cut into as many pieces as you need (which should be approx 10 - 12). You must dip the knife into hot water between each cut. Decorate with chocolate curls.

Clafoutis

Serves 8

900g / 2lbs soft fruit black cherries are traditional

50g / 2oz plain flour

Pinch of salt

50g / 2oz caster sugar

3 eggs

300ml / ¹/₂ pt. milk

1 tbsp oil

A doctor we know who is a Waitrose devotee says this is the best. So we did what the doctor ordered, tried it and loved it.

Butter a shallow ovenproof dish and fill with the soft fruit. In a blender or Magimix, blend the flour, salt, sugar, eggs, milk and oil to make a batter.

Pour this batter over the fruit (make sure it is covered).   Bake for 40 - 45 minutes at 180°C/350°F/Gas 4 then lower heat to 150°C/300°F/Gas 2 for about 15 minutes until it looks brown and when pierced with a knife the knife comes out clean.

Serve warm, dusted with icing sugar.

Keith recommends
French sweet Monbazillac

GrAnnie's Swedish Apple Cáke

Serves 12

700g / 1¹/₂lbs white breadcrumbs

225g / 8oz butter

225g / 8oz demerara sugar

8 medium cooking apples stewed with a little sugar

Chocolate for grating on top (optional)

This recipe has always been called Swedish but I have been reliably informed that there is nothing Swedish about this cake and I probably made it up. However, it is a good no-bake pudding to use up stale bread and windfall apples.

Fry breadcrumbs in butter and sugar until they are crunchy. In a 10 inch/25cm springform tin, make several layers of fried breadcrumbs and stewed apples, starting and finishing with breadcrumbs. Grate the chocolate over the top. Refrigerate and serve with ice cream or cream.

This recipe can be easily halved and put in an 8 inch/20cm tin.

Hazelnut Meringue

Serves 8-10

Meringue

4 large egg whites

250g / 9oz caster sugar

1 tsp cornflour

1 tsp white wine vinegar

1 tsp vanilla extract

100g / 3¹/₂oz Waitrose roasted chopped hazelnuts

Filling

300ml /¹/₂ pt. double cream

1 tbsp drinking chocolate

1 tbsp caster sugar

To decorate

Icing sugar, for dusting

Raspberries

Melted chocolate

Preheat oven to 180°C/350°F/Gas 4. Line two baking trays with baking parchment. Whisk the egg whites in a clean bowl with an electric mixer until stiff. Slowly add the sugar, 1 tablespoon at a time. Fold in the cornflour, white wine vinegar and vanilla essence, followed by the hazelnuts. Divide the mixture between the two trays, spreading to make a circle approx 23cm/9 inch in diameter.

Bake for 35 mins until light brown and crisped. Remove from oven and allow to cool on the trays. For the filling, whisk all the ingredients together until softly whipped. Use to sandwich the two layers together. To serve, dust the top of the meringue with sieved icing sugar and decorate, if liked, with raspberries and drizzled chocolate.

Palobo

6 eggs

110g / 4oz milk chocolate

225g / 8oz good dark chocolate

175g / 6oz caster sugar

175g / 6oz butter

This is a highly calorific revenge on the thin brigade, but if you can get them to try it, those stick insects will be converted.

Melt chocolate and butter in bowl over hot water. Separate eggs. Beat yolks and sugar until light and fluffy. Add the chocolate and butter mixture to the yolks and sugar mixture Whisk whites until really stiff and fold into mixture. Pour into a bowl and put in fridge to set.

Note: contains raw eggs

Rocky Mountain Crumble

Serves 4

700g / 1½ lbs of lightly cooked seasonal fruit

Crumble topping;

25g / 1oz rolled oats

25g / 1oz powdered milk

50g / 2oz plain flour

100g / 3½ oz butter, chilled chopped into several pieces

75g / 3oz light soft brown sugar

A John Lewis and Waitrose fan, Morag was one of our favourite customers when we had the café. We persuaded her to reveal the recipe of this wonderful pudding. Seemingly it is 50 years old, born in Canada and used by generations of her family. Morag says she often doubles or trebles the quantities of the crumble topping and freezes any leftovers in a plastic bag.

It tastes absolutely luscious.

Place all ingredients in a food processor and pulse until combined (you may have to break up the last bit with your fingers).

Sprinkle the crumble topping on the fruit (with not too much added sugar as topping is very sweet.) Bake at 180°C/350°F/Gas Mark 4 for 25 - 30 mins.

Meringue Roulade

Serves 10-12

5 large egg whites

225g / 8oz caster sugar

1 tsp cornflour

1 tsp white wine vinegar

50g / 2oz Waitrose flaked almonds

Icing sugar, for rolling

Filling

300ml / $^1/_2$ pt. double cream

Raspberries, strawberries, passionfruit or lemon curd

Impress your dinner party guests with this pudding. It has the wow factor without the panic.

Preheat oven to 180°C/350°F/Gas 4.
Line the base and sides of a 33cm x 23cm/13 inch x 9 inch Swiss roll tin with baking parchment. Whisk the egg whites until frothy and doubled in bulk. Gradually add the caster sugar and continue to whisk until very stiff and shiny. Fold in the cornflour and vinegar. Pour into the prepared tin and smooth the surface. Scatter almonds over the top and bake for about 40 mins until pale brown and crispy. Leave to cool in the tin, then turn out onto a sheet of baking parchment dusted with icing sugar, then carefully peel off the other piece of baking parchment. Whip the cream until lightly thickened, spread over meringue and then add your chosen filling. Carefully roll the roulade (along the long side), using the baking parchment to help.

Tip
Be brave when rolling it up; it may crack, but the filling will help hold it together!

Cakey Heaven

If this chapter seems that we are majoring on cakes and baking, it is probably because at least one of us is the Queen of cakes and unsurpassable. Those of you who frequent the other coffee shops in Cirencester may recognise some of the cakes in the following pages. That should rest our case that these recipes are foolproof and the cakey public like them – so go and bake and mop up the compliments.

Apricot Flapjacks

Serves 15

225g / 8oz butter

3 heaped tbsp golden syrup

200g / 7oz caster sugar

110g / 4oz self-raising flour

110g / 4oz jumbo oats

175g / 6oz Waitrose own brand cornflakes

175g / 6oz Waitrose dried apricots, chopped

Preheat oven to 200°C/400°F/Gas Mark 6. Line a tin, approx 25cm x 20cm/10 inch x 8 inch, with baking parchment.
Melt the butter and golden syrup in a saucepan, then stir in the remaining ingredients. Spread the mixture about 1cm/½ inch thick in the tin and bake for approx 20 mins, until golden at the edges. Allow to cool in the tin, then cut into squares.

We have both been heard to say that there is no new recipe under the sun, but we have never found this one anywhere else and can confidently claim that Sally invented it. She used to chop up whole apricots meticulously and slowly. When we discovered Waitrose chopped them for her, she was delighted. These flapjacks are not for waist watchers or for the dentally challenged as they are very sweet and very chewy.... local dentists love us. Jane is a huge fan of these calorific bars and would exchange her regular Danish pastry for one of them any day.
Most days she can be found in Waitrose café dispensing advice and gossip to her many friends and asking why there are no apricot flapjacks to buy. We hope she will use this recipe but continue to be the Waitrose agony aunt and enjoy a bacon roll instead.

Baby Boiled Fruit Cakes

150g / 5oz butter

600g / 1lb 4oz mixed fruit

175g / 6oz soft brown sugar

1 tsp mixed spice

1 tsp ground ginger

1 tsp bicarbonate of soda

2 eggs, well beaten

150g / 5oz plain flour

150g / 5oz self-raising flour

Easy-peasy little cakes that earn you undeserved compliments, especially if you ice them and display them on a pretty plate.

Gently melt the first six ingredients then add the next three and be sure to mix well. Pour the mixture (which you will think is too sloppy) into muffin-sized baking cases and cook for 35mins at 170°C/325°F/Gas Mark 4.

Bakewell Tart

Serves 8-10

Base

225g / 8oz sweet pastry or pkt. of ready made

3 tbsp good quality raspberry jam

Frangipane

175g / 6oz butter

175g / 6oz caster sugar

1 tsp almond extract

3 large eggs

175g / 6oz ground almonds

40g / $1^{1}/_{2}$oz self-raising flour

Glacé Icing

175g / 6oz icing sugar

Hot water

25g / 1oz flaked almonds, toasted

Preheat oven to 190°C/375°F/Gas Mark 5. Line a 23cm/9 inch flan tin with the pastry, and spread the jam over the base. Chill in the fridge while you make the filling. Beat together the butter, sugar and almond extract until light and fluffy. Gradually beat in the eggs, then stir in the ground almonds and flour. Spread on top of the jam. Bake for around 30 - 40 mins until golden brown and firm. Allow to cool, then remove from the tin and place on serving plate. For the icing, place the icing sugar in a bowl and add sufficient hot water to make a smooth icing. Spread on top of the tart and sprinkle with toasted flaked almonds.

Variation – Frangipane

To make a delicious tart use the almond mixture but cover with fruit (blueberries, pears or apricots). If using this, it would be better to use apricot jam instead of raspberry on the base of the tart case, and when cooked glaze with warm apricot jam.

Chocolate Brownies

Serves 15

350g / 12oz plain chocolate (50% cocoa solids), broken into pieces

225g / 8oz soft margarine (Stork is best)

225g / 8oz caster sugar

3 large eggs, beaten

1 tsp vanilla extract

2 tsp instant coffee

dissolved in 2 tbsp hot water

110g / 4oz self-raising flour, sieved

75g / 3oz walnuts, finely chopped (can be left out)

Icing sugar, for dusting

Sally is the queen of cakes – she can't fail at any cake, but her Chocolate Brownies are sensational. She tried and tested countless recipes, playing around with various types of chocolate, using more flour, less flour, brown sugar, white sugar, all butter, all margarine…. and this was the winner.

Preheat oven to 180°C/350°F/Gas Mark 4. Line the base and sides of a tin, approx 25cm x 20cm/10 inch x 8 inch, with baking parchment.
Melt the chocolate and margarine in a bowl set over a pan of hot water. Allow to cool slightly. In another bowl, beat together the sugar, eggs, vanilla extract and coffee.

Gradually add the chocolate mixture to the egg mixture. Fold in the flour and walnuts. Pour into the prepared tin. Bake for 35 - 40 mins until firm and a crust has formed – a toothpick/skewer inserted into the centre should come out slightly sticky. Leave to cool in the tin, then cut into squares and dust with sieved icing sugar.

Tip
We use Bournville or Waitrose plain chocolate in this recipe.

Carrot Cake

Serves 8-10

Cake

3 large eggs, beaten

175ml / 6fl oz sunflower oil

50ml / 2fl oz soured cream

2 tsp vanilla extract

175g / 6oz dark muscovado sugar

175g / 6oz light soft brown sugar

250g / 9oz plain wholemeal flour

75g / 3oz desiccated coconut

1 tsp grated nutmeg

2 tsp ground cinnamon

1 tsp bicarbonate of soda

$^1/_2$ tsp salt

300g / 11oz grated carrots

Cream cheese icing

175g / 6oz cream cheese

25g / 1oz butter, softened

110g / 4oz icing sugar, sieved

1 tsp vanilla extract

Carrot cake recipes abound, but the origin of this one is Kiwi and no one has made a dud one yet, some have won prizes with it.

Preheat oven to 180°C/350°F/Gas Mark 4. Line a 23cm/9 inch round cake tin with baking parchment. In a mixing bowl, beat together the eggs, oil, soured cream and vanilla extract, then add the two types of sugar and beat well. Add the remaining dry ingredients (flour, coconut, spices, bicarb and salt), followed by the carrots. Mix very well then pour into the prepared tin. Bake for approx 1 hour until risen and springy in the centre. For the icing, mix all the ingredients together well. When the cake is cold, spread the icing on the top.

Coffee & Walnut Cake

Serves 8

Cake

110g / 4oz softened butter

110g / 4oz softened margarine

225g / 8oz caster sugar

1 tbsp light soft brown sugar

2 tbsp instant coffee dissolved in 5 tbsp boiling water

4 large eggs, beaten

225g / 8oz self-raising flour

50g / 2oz walnuts, finely chopped

Buttercream

110g / 4oz butter, softened

225g / 8oz icing sugar

To decorate

50g / 2oz walnut halves

Our grannies always swore by a "Fullers Coffee and Walnut Cake" but this is better by far, and some would say it is Sally's triumphant signature cake. We have seen genteel women fighting for the last slice!

Preheat oven to 180°C/350°F/Gas Mark 4. Grease 2 x 20 cm/8 inch round cake tins then line the base with baking parchment. For the cake, cream together the butter, margarine and two types of sugar until light and fluffy (ideally in a freestanding mixer for at least 10 mins). Gradually add the beaten eggs with the mixer on slow speed, followed by half the coffee (reserving the other half for the buttercream). Turn the mixer to its lowest speed and add the flour followed by the chopped walnuts. Divide the mixture between the two tins and bake for approx 25 mins or until risen and springy in the centre. Turn out onto a cooling rack and allow to cool. For the buttercream, beat together the softened butter, icing sugar and reserved coffee until light. Fill and top the cooled cake with the buttercream and decorate with the walnut halves.

Florentines

50g / 2oz butter

225g / 8oz caster sugar

25g / 1oz cornflour

300ml / 10fl oz double cream

225g / 8oz Waitrose Flaked almonds

175g / 6oz Waitrose Glacé cherries

50g / 2oz Mixed peel

Angelica (six tiny bits)

200g / 7.5oz bar Waitrose plain chocolate

Melt butter gently with caster sugar. When sugar has dissolved add cornflour, cook for a few minutes on low heat then add the cream. Mix well then throw in the selection of nuts, etc. (do not worry about the proportions, but the almonds are the stars). Drop spoonfuls of the mixture well apart on baking parchment and bake for approximately 15 mins at 170°C/325°F/Gas Mark 3 but look at them often for they are temperamental and will run too easily into a giant Florentine. When cool, spread melted chocolate over one side and leave to cool.

Tip: Kept in Tupperware in the freezer is best – eat straight from freezer, never gets stale.

Florentines for cranks

(ie. The "no wheat brigade" - we all have them in our families.)

3 egg whites

150g / 5oz icing sugar

375g / 13oz flaked almonds

Zest of two oranges

Mix all the ingredients together very well. Spoon mixture on to baking parchment well apart and flatten with a wet fork.   Bake at 170°C/325°F/Gas Mark 3 for 15 mins or until nicely browned around the edges and firm enough to lift on to a cooling rack.

Heavenly Bars

Serves 15 slices

*200g / 7oz plain chocolate
(approx 50% cocoa solids),
melted*

100g / 3¹/₂oz butter

200g / 7oz caster sugar

2 large eggs, beaten

*200g / 7oz desiccated
coconut*

100g / 3¹/₂oz raisins

*100g / 3¹/₂oz chopped
glacé cherries*

This aptly named slice is for the no-wheat brigade, but it is so good that ordinary mortals devour it.

Line a 25cm x 20cm/10 inch x 8 inch tin with baking parchment.
Pour the melted chocolate into the prepared tin and spread evenly over the base. Allow to set for about 1 hour.
Preheat oven to 180°C/350°F/Gas Mark 4. Beat the butter and the sugar until pale, then slowly add the eggs. Mix in the coconut followed by the raisins and cherries. Spoon over the set chocolate and bake for 30 - 35 mins until golden. Leave to cool in the tin, then cut into squares.

Tip
We use Waitrose plain chocolate for this recipe.

Meringues

6 egg whites

350g / 12oz caster sugar

1 tbsp cornflour

1 tbsp raspberry vinegar
(raspberry not vital, can use
white wine vinegar)

When you have made crème bruleé, or whenever you have egg whites begging to be used, always go for a batch of meringues - they are easy to make despite their diva-ish reputation, they keep for ever in your airing cupboard, freezer or air-tight Tupperware and if they get knocked about a bit, turn them into Eton mess. Hard-and-fast rule, 2 oz caster sugar to one egg white.

In a clean, dry mixing bowl whisk the whites until they do not fall out of the bowl when inverted (show-off trick for children) or, much safer, when they are stiff and look like clouds. Add sugar gradually, beat well between additions and then fold in cornflour and

vinegar. Pipe if you are neat like Sally or dollop if like Annie onto baking parchment and bake for 2 hours at 80°C/175°F/Gas Mark 1/4. Sandwich together with whipped cream (flavour with cocoa if you fancy) – this mixture also makes tons of mini-meringues that look really good piled up and studded with raspberries for an occasion.

Mrs Foster's Thing

Makes 15 slices

110g / 4oz butter

2 heaped tbsp golden syrup

2 tbsp light soft brown sugar

1 heaped tbsp drinking chocolate

110g / 4oz raisins

350g / 12oz digestive biscuits, crushed

Topping

110g / 4oz plain (50% cocoa solids) chocolate, chopped

Granny Annie's granny's cook claimed to be the "inventor" of Mrs Foster's thing. She was called Mrs Foster, but we suspect that is where the truth ends.

Line the base and sides of a tin, approx 25cm x 20cm/10 inch x 8 inch, with baking parchment. Place the butter, golden syrup, sugar and drinking chocolate in a medium saucepan. Melt over a gentle heat, stirring to combine. Off the heat, add the raisins and the biscuits. Leave to set. For the topping, melt the chocolate in a bowl over a pan of hot water, or microwave on the defrost setting. Pour over the set mixture and allow to harden before cutting.

Tip

Never be tempted to use cheap cooking chocolate (Mrs Foster would turn in her grave!); we use Waitrose plain chocolate.

Best Ever Cherry Cake

110g / 4oz soft margarine

110g / 4oz caster sugar

110g / 4oz glacé cherries (cut in halves)

100g / 3¹/₂oz self-raising flour

110g / 4oz ground almonds

2 eggs (already beaten)

Mrs May makes the best cherry cake we have ever tasted or cooked.   By that we mean the cherries never ever sink and everyone has two slices.   She is an enchanting character who, with her husband, shops at Cirencester Waitrose every other Wednesday (always buying Waitrose cherries for the famous cake). She and Mr May live in Tewkesbury and they have to pass two other Waitrose stores to get to the Cirencester branch – so what does that say about the store?   Thank you Mrs May.

Beat all the ingredients together (except the cherries) until well combined. Then fold in the cherries and put into a 1lb lined loaf tin and bake for 50 - 60 mins at 150°C/300°F/Gas Mark 2.

Orange and Almond Cake

Serves 8-10

Cake

50g / 2oz stale white breadcrumbs

200g / 7oz caster sugar

100g / 3¹/₂oz ground almonds

1¹/₂ tsp baking powder

200ml / 7fl oz sunflower oil

4 large eggs

Grated rind of 1 large orange

Grated rind of ¹/₂ lemon

To decorate

25g / 1oz toasted flaked almonds (optional)

Syrup

Juice of 1 orange

Juice of ¹/₂ lemon

75g / 3oz caster or granulated sugar

3 cloves

Pinch of cinnamon or 1 cinnamon stick

Line the base of a 20 cm/8 inch round deep cake tin with baking parchment.
Mix the breadcrumbs, sugar, ground almonds and baking powder in a bowl. Whisk the oil with the eggs and pour onto the dry ingredients. Add the grated rind and mix well. Pour into the prepared tin and place in a cold oven. Turn the temperature to 180°C/350°F/Gas Mark 4 and bake for 45 - 50 mins or until golden. Meanwhile make the syrup: place all the ingredients in a pan and bring to the boil, stirring occasionally. Simmer for 5 mins until syrupy. When the cake is cooked, leave it in the tin to cool, then turn out onto a serving plate and spoon the syrup over. Decorate with toasted flaked almonds, if liked.

This Sophie Grigson inspired recipe is fantastic served as a pudding with a dollop of crème fraîche.

Rachel's Favourite Chocolate Cake

Cake

225g / 8oz dark chocolate

225g / 8oz butter

275g / 10oz dark brown sugar

110g / 4oz fresh white breadcrumbs

110g / 4oz ground almonds

6 eggs, separated (whites stiffly beaten)

Butter icing

75g / 3oz butter (softened)

175g / 6oz icing sugar

1 heaped tbsp cocoa.

2 tbsp ganache (taken from below)

Mix all of the ingredients well with two tbsp of hot water.

Ganache

200g / 7.5oz Waitrose plain chocolate

200 ml. / 7.5fl oz double cream

Melt slowly on a low heat and when cool pour over the cakes.

This is delicious and rich and keeps well for several days, except it never lasts that long as it is so more-ish.

For the cake melt the chocolate with 11 tablespoons of water, allow to cool. Beat butter and sugar together until soft. Add egg yolks, almonds and breadcrumbs. Mix in melted chocolate and fold in the egg whites. Put into two 20cm / 8 inch lined cake tins and cook for approximately 35 - 40 mins at 180°C/350°F/ Gas Mark 4. Take out and leave to cool in their tins then turn out onto a rack. Sandwich together with butter icing and cover with ganache.

Rocky Road

200g / 7oz Waitrose plain dark chocolate

100g / 3¹/₂oz Waitrose milk chocolate

125g / 4¹/₂oz butter

1 generous tbsp golden syrup

100g / 3¹/₂oz digestive biscuits

100g / 3¹/₂oz rich tea biscuits

100g / 3¹/₂oz marshmallows (mini if possible)

This ubiquitous slice makes no gesture to the slimmers, although we have seen them sneaking a bite or two. We have played around with lots of combinations of ingredients - it is a good-tempered treat that needs no baking. Here is our version.

Melt chocolates and butter with golden syrup in a large bowl. Bash the biscuits with a rolling pin and under no circumstance put in Magimix! Add cut up marshmallows (if you cannot get the mini version). When butter, syrup and chocolate mix is melted, combine with biscuits and marshmallows then put into a lined tin 20cm x 20cm (8 inch x 8 inch) in fridge. Cut into squares when set. We sometimes drizzle white chocolate randomly over the top when set, but this is really gilding the lily.

Scones

Serves 8

225g / 8oz self-raising flour

¹/₂ tsp baking powder

50g / 2oz butter

25g / 1oz caster sugar

*1 egg, made up to 150ml /
¹/₄ pt with milk or buttermilk*

Scones are the cornerstone of any tea time, especially when served with some delicious jam and clotted cream. But they don't keep.... so eat them as fresh as possible.

Preheat oven to 200°C/400°F/Gas Mark 6. Line a baking sheet with baking parchment. Sift the flour and baking powder into a large mixing bowl. Rub in the butter until the mixture resembles fine breadcrumbs (you can use a freestanding mixer). Stir in the sugar. Beat together the egg and milk/buttermilk and add most of the liquid to the rubbed-in mixture. Mix to form a soft (but not sticky) dough, adding more liquid as necessary.

Turn out onto a floured surface and roll or press out to a thickness of 2cm/3/4 inch. Cut into rounds with a 5cm/2 inch cutter and brush the tops with any liquid left in the jug. Bake for 15 - 20 mins until pale golden. Transfer to a wire rack to cool.

Variation – Fruit Scones
Add 50g / 2oz sultanas after the sugar.

Shortbread

275g / 10oz soft butter

125g / 4oz caster sugar

350g / 12oz plain flour

75g / 3oz cornflour

Pinch baking powder

Heat oven to 170°C/325°F/Gas Mark 4.

Blend the butter and sugar. Add sieved dry
ingredients and put into lined tin –
a 10 inch circular tin is a good size.
Bake for 20 - 25 minutes or until
lightly golden.

You can use this mixture to make
biscuits, but they will cook in no time so
be careful. We often dip half the
biscuit into melted chocolate and let set
on baking parchment.

TIP
2 tbsp of chopped crystallised ginger
mixed in makes a lovely change.

Versatile Victoria Sponge

Serves 8

Cake

110g / 4oz softened butter

110g / 4oz softened margarine

240g / 8¹/₂oz caster sugar

4 large eggs, beaten

225g / 8oz self-raising flour

Filling 1

Buttercream (175g / 6oz icing sugar and 75g / 3oz butter, beaten well)

Good quality jam

Filling 2

Fresh cream

Lemon curd

Raspberries

Preheat oven to 180°C/350°F/Gas Mark 4. Grease 2 x 20 cm/8 inch round cake tins then line the base with baking parchment. Beat the butter and margarine with the sugar until light and fluffy (ideally in a freestanding mixer for at least 10 mins). Gradually add the beaten eggs with the mixer on slow speed. Then turn the mixer to its lowest speed and add the flour. Divide the mixture between the two tins. Bake for 20 - 25 mins until golden and springy in the centre. Allow to cool completely before filling with either of the suggested fillings.

Variation – Fairy Cakes
Follow the recipe and method above, but use to fill 15 muffin cases in standard muffin tins. Bake for 15 - 20 mins until golden. Allow to cool completely before decorating with glacé icing (made with 225g / 8oz icing sugar and a little hot water) and sweets, such as Smarties or Dolly Mixtures.

If you want to use this basic recipe for a chocolate cake, swap 2oz (50g) of self raising flour for 2oz (50g) of cocoa. A really useful tip to keep the chocolate cake moist for much longer is to stir in, at the last minute, one tablespoon of Golden Syrup. Fill and top with chocolate butter cream and ganache (as with Rachel's chocolate cake page 56)

Party Party

We hope this chapter will help you enjoy your own party. Planning and organisation are the keys and with a few tips and cheats, the party and you will be a success. Most of you will have your own lunch and dinner party recipes, but we are asked most often for our canapé recipes; how many to serve, on what and how many choices to offer. So read on and enjoy your party.

Quantities

A lot of different factors play a part in this; time of day, time of party, the season and who are your guests. For example, if you are giving a charity party and people have paid, they will expect and eat much more, but the following are just general pointers and not rules.

A good yardstick is that you should serve about 5 or 6 pieces per person for the first hour of a party and after that about 4 or 5.

If the party is to be all canapés, a greedy guest will expect about 15 bites. The women, usually on diets, will take less to start with. If serving the canapés before a dinner, allow 4 to 5 per guest.
Hot canapés often overshadow the cold ones especially in the cooler seasons, so hold them back until the party is in full swing.

Be inventive with your serving, e.g. sausages can be served in a hollowed out loaf, decorate with flowers and use interesting plates.

Remember that Waitrose hire out glasses and fish kettles without charge, just give them good notice.

Easiest of all, and never underestimate them, are quails' eggs and smoked salmon. They are the hostesses' Valium and require very little attention and can be ready for the guests who arrive too early.

Quails' Eggs – We serve these in a little basket to resemble a nest and serve celery salt on the side (picture) but they can be offered with a number of dips e.g. cumin, spiced salts or sweet chilli sauce.

Smoked Salmon – Serve it on blinis (Waitrose sell these) with crème fraîche and mock caviar, or on rye bread that you have cut into small bite-sized rounds. Make cigarette-like rolls of it and fill with dill flavoured cream cheese – the possibilities are endless – long live smoked salmon.

Parmesan Biscuits

These little sweethearts can be eaten by themselves or used as a base and topped with roasted baby tomato and mozzarella. Whatever, they are a good thing to keep in an airtight tin. One of our husbands says "No house should be without them". He can't cook.

110g / 4oz plain flour

Salt , cayenne

75g / 3oz butter, softened

110g / 4oz grated parmesan

Combine in Magimix, cut into shapes – we do stars for Christmas. Bake for 10 minutes at 180°C/350°F/Gas Mark 4.

Variations:
Add 1 tsp dried thyme or rosemary to mix, or 1 tsp chopped black olives.

Mushroom Tarts
With Hollandaise

175g / 6oz chestnut mushrooms, finely chopped

4 spring onions, finely chopped

1 tbsp red wine

25g / 1oz butter

Fresh thyme

*Savoury tart cases
(make your own or use Croustades from the store)*

Hollandaise sauce (Waitrose is fine)

Sauté the mushrooms and spring onions in the butter in a frying pan with the red wine and thyme until soft and all the moisture has evaporated. Allow to cool slightly and add to cases. Top with a little hollandaise, warm through in the oven and serve.

Lollipops

20 baby tomatoes

1 pkt mini mozzarella balls

Pesto (fresh is best)

Chopped parsley and basil combined

Cut tomatoes in half and scoop out seeds and flesh. Put a dab of pesto in the bottom of the tomato. Spear the tomato on a long stick. Push the mozzarella ball into the tomato shell. Dip in chopped herbs and serve in a glass vase.

Fresh Tuna & Watermelon

Watermelon

Fresh tuna

Chilli sauce

Avoiding the black seeds, make balls of watermelon (if you have a melon baller, if not just chop into cubes). Flash fry tuna and set aside to cool. Try to get equal-sized cubes of melon and tuna, then thread onto longish sticks.
Serve with a small bowl of chilli sauce.

Spoons

Suggestions

Prawns in chilli sauce (Sharwood's)

Diced cucumber in chilli sauce

Smoked fish mousse

Kedgeree

Risotto

Coronation chicken

We like using spoons – they are a good vehicle for many fillings. Our friend Gabi gets us wonderful Chinese spoons from a restaurant in Bristol and they look wonderful on a pretty plate. You don't have to serve Chinese bits on them; see the suggestions.

Mini Meals

We had a craze for doing mini meals as canapés and although sometimes fiddly they are very impressive. Here are a few suggestions:

For these "wow catchers" we make little breadbaskets which keep for days in an airtight tin. Then fill them with meals such as scrambled egg and bacon breakfasts, Christmas lunches, or fish pie mixture.

Makes about 24 baskets:
1 loaf white sliced bread
Olive oil – about 3 tbsp but may be more

Roll out the slices of bread with a rolling pin so they are thin and malleable, then cut out with a cutter.   Brush both sides of the rounds with oil and push into the holes of two 12-hole patty tins (the ones you use for mince pies).   Bake at 180°C/350°F/Gas Mark 4 for 10 minutes or until crisp.   Cool and store if you are cooking ahead.

Mini Caesar Salads

Little Gems

Anchovies

Parmesan shavings

Tiny croutons

Caesar dressing (use readymade unless you are purist, in which case you will know how to make it)

Break up the Little Gems and use as your base for the filling. Add small cubes of bread that you have fried or baked and add shavings of parmesan. Not everyone likes anchovies, so be sure to leave some without. Pour a little dressing on at the last minute.

Mini Bangers & Mash

*1 pkt. of Cocktail sausages
(Waitrose are best)*

4 tbsp mashed potato

Salt and pepper

Grated parmesan

Cook sausages – grill or bake until brown. Allow to become cold as they are easier to slit. Put well-seasoned (and no lumps) mash into a piping bag with a narrow nozzle (you can use a spoon if, like us, you can't locate the right nozzle). Make a slit down the length of the sausage and fill with the mash. Sprinkle with cheese (optional). Heat in pre-heated oven for about 10 mins.

Just Sausages *always a Winner*

Cook sausages as for mini bangers and mash, but while hot cover with either:

Honey and mustard

Honey and mint jelly

Honey, soy sauce and sesame seeds

Serve on sticks – they look good in a hollowed-out loaf

And don't knock the ubiquitous devils on horseback either (prunes wrapped in streaky bacon and baked in the oven).

Shot Glasses

Another handy vehicle at canapé time when you are bored with conventional bases.

We use them to offer cold soup in the summer (pea and mint, or gazpacho). Lately, in retro mood, we have served shrimp cocktail in them with tiny spoons. We've even made mini trifles or chocolate mousse to serve at the end of a canapé party.

Specialist Counters

Every Waitrose has its experts at its fresh counters and wine section.

Known as 'Specialists,' they are recognisable by their distinctive black aprons.

All have been highly trained, gaining national certificates, with most having

had a fascinating journey to their post.

WaitroseSpecialist

Vanessa & Cheese Stories

Vanessa is the big cheese of the cheese section who astonished us with her knowledge. Trained by the Specialist Cheese Council, her tales of the provenance of many of the cheeses are wonderful - some of which can be illustrated by her choice of cheeses for the new 'ideal cheeseboard' that we commissioned her to create.

She told us how Reblochon began life as a tactic to fool the taxman when collecting his dues based on the milk yield – they held back and had a second milking and made the cheese from it. "Reblochon" comes from the verb reblocher, which means "to pinch the udder a second time".

We had a wonderful time at a farm in Leonard Stanley, owned by Liz and Brian Godsell. The farm has evolved from Granny Godsells' brewery, through arable and, in the 1980s, Liz's father started a dairy herd that still serves the cheese plant today. Vanessa has also been to the farm to see the whole process of Single Gloucester being made from a mixture of full cream and semi-skimmed milk from their herd of Severn Vale Cattle. You can see and buy the Godsells' cheese at local farmers' markets and, of course, at Vanessa's kingdom in Waitrose. Say it aloud and you will realise that "God sells cheese" is a strapline that would be the envy of any copywriter.

The couple who now turn out countless cheeses are a story in themselves.   It is Liz's side of the family and although the only daughter, and despite two sceptical brothers and father, she was determined to work on the farm.   She had met Brian, a geography graduate, at university and he must be one of the few men who can multitask as well as any woman; he has been househusband, housefather and geography teacher until seven years ago.   Then Liz qualified as a Master Cheesemaker, using the milk from their own herd – their cheeses have been a resounding success far beyond Gloucestershire and long may they last.

The Cheeseboard

1. Godsells' Single Gloucester - local cheese, better on cheeseboard than a cooking cheese.

2. Cerney goats cheese - another local cheese made by Avril in a tiny cottage in North Cerney. The pyramid cheese is mild and zingy.

3. Cornish Blue - made on Bodmin Moor. The damp mild climate is ideal for this Gorgonzola-type cheese.

4. Berthaut's Epoisses – best cheese to come out of France, says Vanessa. Dates back to AD960 when the monks made it to eat during fasts when meat was forbidden.

5. Cropwell Bishop White Stilton with Apricots – creamy, sweet and produced by the Skelles family, who are renowned for producing the best Stilton made from milk from local farms in the Vale of Belvoir.

Photo Phillip Hall

Fish
Counter

Photo Phillip Hall

Graham is the Neptune of the fish counter - and the history of his journey is fascinating. He was celebrating fourteen years at Waitrose when we talked to him and took this great photograph. Previously a highly qualified Quantity Surveyor, he came to Waitrose one Christmas after a longish break from surveying. That temporary Christmas job was his rite of passage through various departments, to where he now reigns supreme. We asked him about any interesting customers, and he mentioned a gentleman who regularly bought one, yes one, mussel - he had a pet seahorse that was partial to the mollusc

Fish Counter
Mussels & Chips

Serves 4 or 2 greedy people

1kg / 2lbs 4oz fresh live mussels

300ml / ¹/₂ pt. double cream

2 medium sized glasses of white wine

75g / 3oz Fourme d'ambert cheese for cooking and to crumble over the top

4 shallots

2 cloves garlic

Parsley

Mel has been our invaluable liaison officer during the hectic period of producing this book. We conceived the idea about the time Mel conceived her baby. She is often to be seen as "Graham's Girl" and has aptly given us a fishy recipe.

Finely chop shallots and garlic and fry until soft in a heavy based pan. Add the wine and reduce by at least half. Add the cream and allow to reduce and thicken. Crumble in the cheese and stir until melted. Throw in the mussels, stir, cover and leave for 3 - 5 mins until open. Sprinkle the parsley and the last of the cheese over the top. Serve with home-made chips sprinkled with chopped garlic.

TIP

Discard any mussels that haven't opened.

Meat Counter
Burgundy Beef

Serves 8

1.75kg / 3$^1/_2$ lbs Aberdeen Angus sliced braising steak from the meat service counter

50g / 2oz butter

4 tbsp oil

3 onions, chopped

6 cloves garlic, crushed

200g / 7oz pack lightly smoked bacon lardons

4 tbsp plain flour

75cl bottle Burgundy or other medium to full bodied red wine (Cuvée Chasseur)

1 can anchovy fillets in olive oil, drained and chopped (optional)

400g / 14oz button mushrooms

20g pack flat-leaf parsley, chopped, plus extra to garnish

The secret of this succulent and delicious casserole is to thoroughly sear the beef first in small batches, before adding the other ingredients. The anchovies, although barely detectable, give the beef a rich flavour.

Jeanette brings sunshine to the meat counter with her great smile. For 2 years she has been laying out her wares with style and panache. Her meat knowledge is formidable for someone who came from a desk to manage this large section of the store. All the Waitrose specialists are trained by independent tutors and Jeanette enjoyed training in Newmarket and Dovecote Park. We have seen her sell two sausages to a pensioner with as much care as when a rich and grand customer bought whole fillets of beef. We wanted her favourite meat recipe and here it is – we tasted it, loved it and highly recommend it.

Preheat the oven to 170°C/325°F/Gas Mark 3. Pat the beef dry on kitchen paper and cut into chunky pieces. Melt half the butter and half the oil in a large frying pan and fry a handful of the beef for 3 - 4 minutes, stirring until the meat is thoroughly browned. Drain with a slotted spoon and transfer to a large casserole dish. Fry the remaining meat in small batches, adding a little more oil, as necessary. Transfer to the casserole dish. Add the onions and remaining oil to the pan and fry gently for 5 minutes until beginning to brown. Add the garlic and bacon and fry for a further 2 minutes then stir in the flour and cook for 1 minute.

Gradually pour the wine into the frying pan and bring almost to the boil, stirring often. Add the anchovy fillets and pour over the meat. Cover with a lid and cook in the oven for 1$^1/_2$ hours or until the meat is tender. Meanwhile fry the mushrooms in the remaining butter until softened. Add to the casserole dish with any pan juices and the parsley. Season and cook for a further 10 minutes. Serve, sprinkled with extra parsley.

Wine Specialist
Shoulder of Lamb

Serves 6-8

1 shoulder of lamb

1 whole garlic – cut across middle of bulb

Sprigs of rosemary (or dried)

Tin of anchovies (chopped up)

2oz soft butter

1 glass red wine

1 tbsp redcurrant jelly

We had to wait some time to take this great photograph of Keith because he had only just qualified when we began this book and he was waiting for his tie which is the badge of honour – well done, Keith. He claims to have the best job in the store and most would agree with him. Few customers come to complain – they usually want advice and are often in party mood. If they weren't, we defy them not to be cheered by Keith's unfailing good temper and banter.

Coming from a family-run car business, Keith is another Partner who has had an interesting journey to his 'King of Wine' role. He's been with Waitrose for ten years, starting out on the night shift. By all accounts, at the time, Keith was a food and wine novice, but he soon began his love of cooking whilst home alone in the day after his night's toil. He is married to Margaret, a wonderful matriarch, and head of catering here in Waitrose Cirencester. We loved hearing about her journey from Saturday girl to Section Manager. Having met at Keith's dad's garage, it seems that both have travelled from motors to management.

Keith invented the roast lamb recipe but later saw it on television being executed by a more famous chef.

Make a paste of the garlic, rosemary, anchovies and butter – smear over the lamb. Loosely cover the joint in foil.   Cook in a very moderate oven for about four hours. Open, stand back and smell.

Deglaze the roasting pan with some red wine and the redcurrant jelly and you have a delicious gravy, or "jus" if you want to sound grand.

Green Discs

We must all wonder, as we stand and ponder which box to put our green disc in, who and what benefits from our decision. We decided to pick two very local recipients and ask them how they came to be chosen. It works like this:

In each store there is a syndicate made of a number of Partners who choose which causes to put forward from a fairly long list of hopefuls nominated by customers. It isn't just the share of the monthly £1,000 donation that benefits them. It brings publicity and therefore more awareness and more money. We liked to think that those little green discs were counted one-by-one by some poor person counting out until midnight – not so; they are weighed and divided proportionately

Hope For Tomorrow

This was our first meeting with a green disc recipient, but our directions to its headquarters could not prepare us for the impact of this charity: a narrow, winding country lane and a five-bar gate and cattle grid doesn't presage a vital inspiring concept embodied in the petite human form of Christine Mills, who founded "Hope for Tomorrow" in 2003 after losing her husband to cancer. She, Belinda and Tracy are housed in a busy office annexe to Christine's house. They are dedicated to alleviating some of the stress and difficulties for cancer patients by bringing chemotherapy to rural areas "nearer to patients' homes" through their mobile chemotherapy unit.

Christine shared this vision of mobile treatments with Dr. Sean Elyan, a consultant oncologist, and with her inspirational drive and some help from Sir Stirling Moss and Lord MacLaurin "Hope for Tomorrow" was born. The first unit was launched in 2007 and has now treated more than 1,500 patients and saved more than 40,000 travelling miles.

There are myriad letters from grateful patients, like the gentleman who described the unit as a "godsend". He had to travel just one mile for his treatment, have it with wonderful staff and then managed to do a half day's work, whereas before a 10-hour round trip would render him wiped out for two days.

The charity has recently launched a new state of the art mobile chemotherapy assessment unit as well as a mobile support vehicle. In a unique partnership, the units are owned by "Hope for Tomorrow" and operated by the Gloucestershire Hospitals NHS Foundation Trust. The highly skilled MCU team is based at Cheltenham General Hospital. The new unit and support vehicle will benefit hundreds more Cotswold patients and if the founder of this charity continues with her extraordinary vision and phenomenal energy, the project should extend to the nation.

Thank Heaven for the likes of Christine Mills.

To learn more about this organisation go online at www.hopefortomorrow.org.uk or telephone 01666 505055.

Cotswold Canals Trust

Photo courtesy of K. Burgin

This charity, whose aim is the regeneration and restoration of the Cotswold Canals, wants to bring two of the country's most historic and picturesque inland waterways back to life. This regeneration would once again link England's two great rivers – the Thames and the Severn.

The Stroudwater Navigation was originally promoted by clothiers in the Stroud valleys who needed to obtain coal cheaply from South Wales, Staffordshire and The Forest of Dean to power their looms. The Thames and Severn Canal Company was formed a few years later to share the good fortunes of the proprietors of The Stroudwater Navigation. The result formed a trade link between England's two great rivers.
The entire route certainly challenged the engineers… 36 miles, 57 locks and a tunnel two miles long!

The Cotswold Canals Trust has spearheaded the restoration since 1972 and, although this charity does not have the same visceral appeal as "Hope for Tomorrow", for sheer human energy and nostalgia it cannot be beaten. The Trust has a huge active volunteer force working on several restoration projects and sections of the canal are now "in water"; the Trust even runs boat trips on some of them. Their ultimate goal is the total restoration of the Cotswold Canals as a navigable route from Saul junction (be sure to visit the Saul Heritage Centre) to the Thames at Lechlade. For sheer spectacular go and see the eight locks at Eastington and all that has been achieved by the devoted volunteers.

Although we all know that these man-made waterways were primarily for industrial freight purposes, they always had natural value for the wildlife and that is an essential element of the restoration today; the wealth of this wildlife is surprising. The banks, towpaths and even the engineering structures are home to many species and a huge range of invertebrates, water-birds, waterside mammals and aquatic flora and should be preserved.

The Trust publishes a quarterly newsletter "The Trow", which goes to all Cotswold Canal members – some 5,550 of them, but new members are always welcome; think on it – I am!

If you wish to join this exciting project and learn more, contact: Tel 01285 643440 www.cotswoldcanal.com

Cotswold Canals Trust
Working for Restoration

What Went Wrong?
and sundry tips

LUMPY WHITE SAUCE (or any sauce really):
Liquid added too quickly to basic roux.
Remedy: use balloon whisk, or if really lumpy, whizz in blender or mixer.

SUNKEN CHERRIES IN CHERRY CAKE:
See Mrs May's recipe, but usually they have sunk because they are too wet.   Remedy: roll in ground almonds or flour. The same is true for other fruit.

LEAKY QUICHES:
Holes in pastry.   Remedy: check lined quiche tin with your spectacles on and paint base with egg white.

CAKE TOO DRY:
Too little butter or too much flour.
Remedy: soak in alcohol and smother with cream.

CAKE CRACKED IN THE MIDDLE:
Oven too hot.   Remedy: disguise with frosting.

REAL COFFEE TOO WEAK:
Remedy: add a teaspoon of instant coffee to pot.

STICKY RICE:
Remedy: rinse thoroughly in warm water – it will separate and fluff up.

EGGS CRACK WHILE BOILING:
Eggs put in pan too cold – should be room temperature.   Remedy: add a few drops of vinegar to water.

ONE EGG SHORT FOR RECIPE AND SHOPS SHUT:
One teaspoon of cornflour may save the day.

BROWN SUGAR LIKE CONCRETE:
(always happening to me)
Place in hot oven until sugar is dry and crumbling – put in blender or bash with a rolling pin.

TOO MUCH FAT IN GRAVY:
Pour liquid through ice cubes into a bowl – the fat will solidify.

"It's a very pleasant experience with very helpful and friendly staff."

"The service is superb. The staff are friendly and knowledgeable."

"Big wide aisles – big wide smiles."

"Because the food is good quality, the staff are friendly and we always receive excellent customer service."

"Stefan's smile."

"Excellent produce with very polite and helpful staff."

"Because it's just THE BEST xx"

Waitrose Partners

The branch manager is extremely proud of his team and their dedication to the service of excellent quality food.

"It is the customers and Partners that make a Waitrose branch special and I believe that the Cirencester branch is very special indeed".

Recipe List

They'll never know

Although this book is a cookery book, it is also about enjoying food and if you haven't got time, cheat. All the goodies in these photographs we bought from the store – who would guess or care? Sally swears by the New York Cheesecake and no one has ever rumbled her (they will now) and Zena confessed at book club that she always tops the lemon tart with sliced peaches, covers them with sugar and then caramelises them with her husband's blowtorch. Remember, the French foodies always buy their puddings from the patisserie.